Neighborhood Wars

Sheila Rollins

Copyright © 2011 Sheila\Rollins

All rights reserved.

ISBN: 0615541968
ISBN-13: 978-0-615-54196-9

TO MY FANTASTIC FIVE

What makes you different, makes you special. You are and always will be my inspiration.

CONTENTS

	Preface	I
1	The Conquerors	4
2	YES!	6
3	Good Times	10
4	The Crushers	13
5	Secret Weapon	16
6	Liberators	19
7	Defeating Damian	21
8	Peace	24

PREFACE

"More than Conquerors, we are Liberators!" That was our motto. We stood for freedom to do whatever we wanted in the neighborhood without the fear of being picked on or bullied. This may not seem like a difficult task, but maintaining peace within a three block radius is much harder than it sounds.

My name is J. That's it, just J- no period. I don't know what my mom was thinking. I constantly get asked what it stands for or have people write it as an initial with a period after it. I often wonder if my mom knew how irritating it would be for me. I wanted so badly to have an answer the next time someone asked.

I wish I could take all the credit for starting the Liberators, but it was formed long ago. In its early years, the group called themselves the Conquerors. My older brother, Junior, was the Founder and President.

When Junior was eight-years-old, he and two boys from next door would meet regularly in a top-secret, classified location. He told me later that I was to never disclose the location, "NO MATTER WHAT!" Well, he's sixteen-years-old now and too busy with sports and girls(Yuck) to be a full-time officer, so I'm the President.

I make the big decisions now, which means if I want to broadcast our meeting location, I can.

I don't know why it was such a big secret. We met under the trampoline in my yard. There was nothing around to conceal our identities and anyone who happened to walk or drive past could see us underneath.

Who would've thought that our neighborhood would have enough drama to support our cause for this many years?

1 CONQUERORS

Everyone wants to belong to a club as a kid. My brother, Junior, was no different. The problem was that all the "cool kids" were going through this horrible phase where they thought they were too good to associate with anyone else. They never seemed to realize that if everyone thinks they are better than everyone else, there is nobody left to play with.

I don't understand why these kind of people are called "cool kids". Being cool is a term that should be reserved for those who are well-liked by others and these guys didn't seem to have very many qualities to make them likable. Don't tell Junior, but I think he is much cooler than anyone else in the neighborhood.

Since no other clubs in the neighborhood were taking new members, Junior and his two friends began their own. The three friends referred to themselves as the Conquerors. Junior thought of the name to show all other neighborhood groups that it didn't matter if they let the threesome into their clubs or not. They would conquer any problem thrown at them no matter how big.

2   YES!

I will never forget the day it happened. This was the day I had been waiting for my whole life.

I was a five-year-old running through the sprinkler in our backyard. It was one of those super hot Texas evenings in July and no matter how far the sun went down, it never seemed to get cooler.

All of sudden, I heard screams and saw a blur of body parts fly out from under the trampoline. It looked so funny I couldn't help but laugh out loud. The boys were hopping and running in circles like cats chasing their tails. At first, I thought they were just being silly but it didn't take long to realize… while I was laughing with them, they weren't actually laughing at all. They were crying in pain.

Junior yelled at me to go in the house and get our parents for help. Now, I faced a dilemma. You see, I wanted to be a Conqueror for as long as I could remember. Even though I was only five, I wanted to hang out with Junior and his friends, but they thought I was a pest and would only get in the way.

I knew my parents would hear the screams and come running so I had to act fast as to not miss this opportunity. I announced that as soon as they allowed me to be a member of the club, I'd get help.

With no time to spare, I finally heard those two little words I had been waiting to hear for so long… "You're in!"

Immediately after I heard those magical words, the door opened and out ran my parents. I never had time to run in and fetch them, but by then the words were already spoken. You see, in my family, Rule #1 states that if you make a decision to say something you better mean it.

Let me clarify. My Mom asked what we wanted to eat on the way home from baseball practice one day. When she answered my sister's question about where the food would be from, my sister let out a loud groan. After hearing the sound, Mom told her she could eat a peanut butter sandwich when we got home. My sister decided that food from the restaurant would be better than a sandwich from home and tried to change her mind.

After returning home, Mom divided the food in the bag to everyone in the family except for one person. When my sister asked where her food was, Mom opened the pantry and handed her a jar of peanut butter. We don't complain about what is for dinner anymore.

We really only had two rules, but they were huge and covered a lot of territory. As kids, we don't like to talk much about Rule #2. That's the rule that reminds us we better do something the first time we are asked. We knew that if none of us stepped up and volunteered then we would all suffer the consequences.

I remember my parents asking us to vacuum the living room floor after putting up the Christmas Tree one year. They never yelled or nagged so none of us could have predicted what was going to happen.

The next day, we were called to come downstairs. Mom told us each to raise our right hand and repeat after her. So we repeated, " I am a human vacuum cleaner." Before we could mentally process the words coming out of our own mouths, Mom had wrapped duct tape around each raised hand. I'm sure it was quite a sight to see five kids crawling on the floor patting duct tape against the carpet to pick up pine needles. It would have been much easier to step up and volunteer to use the vacuum cleaner.

We learned quickly these two rules would be upheld at all times, and that was that.

So as I stood dripping wet on the porch, with a smile from ear-to-ear, my fellow Conquerors were having fire ants sprayed off them. I was so excited I hadn't even noticed Dad grab the sprinkler and Mom yank shoes and socks off my brother and his friends.

To me this will always be remembered as the day the Conquerors conquered the ants, and I conquered the Conquerors.

3   GOOD TIMES

By the time I was eight years old, the Conquerors were up to six members. After convincing Junior that opening up to younger members could benefit us, we inducted our two younger brothers.

Easton was four years old at the time of his induction. He was in charge of collecting dues, which is really just money we needed to buy sodas from the gas station.

Sometimes we would go days without collecting money because we had a system. All of us would go together to buy our sodas and choose the same flavor from the same shelf in the cooler. After paying, we would return to the trampoline and place all of the soda bottles in a pile in the middle of our circle. Easton would then pass the bottles out to each of us so we never knew who actually bought each one.

As we each held a bottle, an announcement was made and all bottles were opened at the same time. Almost always, we would have a couple bottle caps that read, "free soda" underneath. Since nobody knew who bought those specific bottles, there were no arguments over who would get them. We exchanged the caps for more drinks on our next trip to the gas station and shared whatever amount we could get in hopes that we would receive more winning caps. This would continue until we had no more winners and then it was time to send Easton back to collecting dues to start again.

Dues are usually paid by members of a club, but as Conquerors, with no money except on birthdays, it was easier to send in Easton. The true reason Easton was in charge of collecting dues was because he was so cute and innocent that grown-ups had a hard time telling him "no". He'd almost always sucker our grandparents out of money with just a little hug and that smile of his.

The sixth member of the Conquerors was Rex. He was only two so it took more convincing before Junior would let him in. He'd say, "Rex is too young," or, "He can't do anything but get in the way". I knew Junior and his friends were getting older and becoming interested in other things but I wanted to assure the Conquerors survival if the oldest members were to stop attending meetings.

Convincing the club to let Rex be a member was one of my smartest moves. He was small enough to sneak around undetected.

Daily drills were implemented for Rex so he could practice being stealthy. He was awesome! He didn't understand why he had to do the things we told him, but he always did them without asking any questions.

We tried to rotate his drills between pulling pranks on our sister and sneaking snacks to us. For example, one day we may give Rex a rubber spider and tell him to put it in our sister's shoe, and the next day he may be told to sneak popsicles out to us. No matter what we said, he could do it.

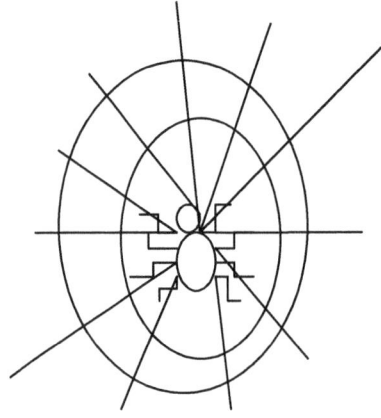

The Conquerors were six members strong and everything worked as planned…until a month ago. Who knew that everything we built over the years was about to change in a period of less than one week?

4   THE CRUSHERS

The three oldest Conquerors, who were now sixteen, loved to shoot baskets by our driveway. I could feel them pulling away more and more in recent months. They were different.

Junior and his friends more frequently wanted to do things that my little brothers couldn't do. Easton was now 6 and Rex was 4. They were constantly told to get out of the way or they would get hurt. I was torn. As the middle child, now ten-years-old, I really wanted to hang out with Junior. I also wanted to have club meetings and continue our Conqueror traditions with Easton and Rex. It wouldn't be long for the decision to be made for me.

I heard a door slam and footsteps running down the hallway. I could hear many different voices at once but could not make out the words. The next thing I knew, my Mom was on the phone explaining that Junior was attacked.

What? Junior? He was one of the best guys I knew. It must have been a mistake.

About five minutes later, I looked out the window to see lights from a police car in the street. There was a group of people around Junior making it impossible for me to see him. I was worried about him and scared. Dad made me stay in the house and it was killing me. This time I would not be able to send Easton or Rex to get information for me. It seemed as if we were all on lockdown.

After about an hour, Junior walked in and went directly to his bedroom. He didn't look at me or speak to me. I realize he didn't feel like talking to anyone but I still took it personally. I loved my brother and hated to see him like that.

I waited until the house was silent and everyone was in bed before I snuck into Junior's room. I knew he would still be awake. That is when I noticed how swollen his eye was and the cut underneath. He looked like a different person but I didn't have the heart to tell him that.

I could tell he didn't want to talk about what happened but once he started the words would not stop pouring out. I felt horrible for him, but at the same time he made me feel special by talking to me about it.

It turned out this big bully on the block behind us was responsible for this attack on my brother and his friends. They had their own club named the Crushers. The Crushers were led by President Damian and claimed they would crush anyone in their path.

Most people stayed as far away from the Crushers as possible. In fact, during the basketball game, Damian and his groupies went out of their way on their bicycles to confront the Conquerors. These were the worst kind of bullies. They jumped off their bikes and told the boys playing basketball to get out of their way because they were trying to ride bikes in that spot.

Junior's eyes filled with water as he explained that there was no time to respond before he felt a sharp pain in his face and something warm trickle down his cheek. He glanced at the corner of his room and I could see the red-stained shirt he was wearing earlier that day.

The police knew exactly who was responsible but by then the Crushers were long gone.

5   SECRET WEAPON

The day following the confrontation with the Crushers, I called an emergency meeting. After waiting for thirty minutes, I realized the three youngest members were the only ones coming.

There was no time to be sad. Easton, Rex, and I had work to do. Ridding the neighborhood of evil-doers was now solely in our hands. The police had been unable to locate Damian; therefore, for our brother's honor and safety and to take back the neighborhood, we knew what we had to do.

We had to not only locate Damian, but also assure he is apprehended. The plan would take my brains, Easton's innocent looks, and Rex's sneakiness and stealth. There was only one problem left. We needed to convince one more person to help us. Someone with the physical strength to bring the Crusher's down since Junior had always been the muscle of our group.

There was only one kid in the whole neighborhood mean enough and scary enough to take on the Crushers. The toughest kid around and we lived in the same house. This was not going to be easy, but it was time to bring in our secret weapon. It was time to bring in… our sister.

There is nothing scarier than a fourteen-year-old girl. I believe the reason Rex is so good at sneaking around is because he was scared our sister would kill him if she ever caught him.

The three of us walked down the hall towards Brooke's room. The closer we got to the big "Do Not Enter" sign, the slower we walked. I could hear that the air conditioner was on yet I was dripping with sweat.

Since Rex was the youngest, we made him knock. We had apparently trained him too well because immediately after he knocked, he snuck behind us and left me to do the talking.

Brooke slung the door open and asked what we wanted, and not in a nice way. As the brain of the operation, I began to explain. She looked as if she could not have cared less. She told us she did not have time for our silly schemes. My brain was beginning to hurt so it was Easton's turn. He begged her for help and batted his big blue eyes at her. For a moment I thought she was beginning to break. Wishful thinking, I guess.

Rex had disappeared sometime during our pleading when nobody had noticed. Now he again stood by the door with a guilty look on his face. We grabbed his hand to make sure he stayed with us as we regrouped back at the trampoline.

Easton and I looked at each other with disappointment. How would we ever be able to do this by ourselves? As we sat in silence, we heard the door close and Brooke appeared. We were shocked and a little scared. Our sister never came to our meetings. In fact, she told us repeatedly how dumb they were as she jumped on the trampoline trying to bop us in the head as we sat underneath. Yet, there she was.

Brooke opened her favorite kind of chocolate bar and split it between us. We ate cautiously not knowing if it was poisoned. I did not understand her change of heart but was very thankful for it. I learned not to ask God why, but rather accept and be thankful for the blessings given me. She sat with us under the trampoline and asked where we should start.

Neighborhood Wars

6 LIBERATORS

As we devised our plan to take down Damian, we came to a realization. We were now a completely new group of members than when the Conquerors began. A new group that needed a new name.

Up to this point, we stood for conquering anything that stood in our way of having fun. Our focus had now changed. We wanted the freedom to be able to play in front of our own homes without fearing for our safety. We were more than Conquerors. We were Liberators!

The newly formed Liberators used a stick to sketch our plans in the dirt where grass had stopped growing under the trampoline long ago. We tried our best to cover any scenario that could occur, then began collecting items we would need to put our plans into action.

That night, every hour or so, I'd awake wondering what if our plan didn't work? What if we can't even find

Damian? What it we get hurt? But if there's one thing I knew for sure, our sister was not going to let anyone hurt us, unless it is her.

There was one moment during the night, when I could hear the neighbors across the street yelling at one another. It was loud enough to cause all the dogs on the block to bark. I remember thinking the grown-ups needed to start their own club to spread peace.

It seemed like forever before morning arrived. At breakfast glances were passed, but not much talk. No time for talk, we had work to do.

7 DEFEATING DAMIAN

For two days, the four members of the Liberators rotated shifts as lookouts. We knew Damian lived behind us and he would eventually have to return home for clothes, food, money, or maybe even a bath. We believed he had been hiding out at different kid's houses. Kids that did not have a support system, like the Liberators, to prevent them from buying into Damian's slippery web.

As time passed, we became tired but also more determined. We would not give up no matter what. Junior was our oldest brother, and as a family, the five of us were a team.

Finally on day three, the time came to move. It was lunchtime under the trampoline. As we ate our sandwiches, we heard a popping sound. We immediately recognized the sound of the poppers we saved from the Fourth of July. Rex had snuck them all over in Damian's backyard one day as Easton offered to sell candy at the front door to Damian's mother. We knew Damian had finally stepped on them.

It took a minute to sink in that this was actually happening. Brooke peeked through the fence and verified it really was who we thought, Damian. We knew what we had to do and were prepared to do it.

As soon as Brooke gave the signal that Damian was inside his house, we took our positions and waited patiently.

About twenty minutes later, Damian returned outside. We knew he would exit the back of his house to prevent being spotted by police.

Just as his screen door banged shut, Easton began to work his magic. He was braver than I had ever seen him. With no fear in his voice, he called to Damian and asked if he wanted to buy some lemonade for 50 cents. Damian marched to the fence and grabbed the cup. He said he didn't have to pay, he'd just take it for free. He never noticed Brooke in the tree above them.

Before Damian had a chance to leave, Brooke dropped a rope around him. As she pulled on the rope to tighten it, she slipped and landed in the swimming pool. If we let Damian escape we may never get another chance to catch him. I had to think fast. I could see the rope dangling over the tree branch but it was too high for anyone other than Brooke to reach. I quickly climbed on the trampoline and began to jump higher and higher until I could feel the rope in my hands. As I grabbed the rope and hung, it pulled tightly around Damian. I held on with all my might while Brooke, Easton, and Rex cheered me on.

All of a sudden, I heard Junior's voice. He came running around the corner when he heard the commotion. With a confused expression on his face, he pulled Brooke from the pool. The two of them took the rope from my hands in the knick of time. I did not tell them, but I would not have been able to hold on much longer. I could feel blisters forming on my hands as I dangled from the rope in mid-air.

Rex came running with the cellular phone he had snuck off the kitchen counter. He handed it to Easton to call the police. The police were in awe to see what we had done. Before they took Damian away, they explained to us that we could have really gotten hurt. We all knew the officers were right, but we also knew that if we stuck together there was nothing we could not do.

8 PEACE

I called one more meeting after dinner to discuss the events of the day. At exactly 7:30p.m., I crawled under the trampoline. I was disappointed to see only the three youngest members in attendance once again.

Just as we began the meeting, I heard giggling. I looked over to see Junior, Brooke, Mom, and Dad crawling under the trampoline. This time I was the person who was confused. I had never seen our meetings so crowded.

Mom and Dad said this was a meeting we should all participate in. They were proud of us for pulling together to protect each other. They were also disappointed we had not discussed our plans with them but were relieved nobody was hurt.

When it was Junior's turn to talk he expressed he had no idea what we were scheming and couldn't believe what all we did just for him. I told him he had been a great big brother to us and it was our turn to do something for him.

Brooke was a completely different person to me now than she used to be. I see her in a different light. It must be hard for her to be the only girl in a family with four brothers. I asked her why she ever decided to help us in the first place. She asked if I remembered the chocolate she shared at her first meeting. Of course I did, it was her favorite. The kind she never shared. She explained how after she saw how sad our faces looked as we left her room, she leaned back on her bed and felt a lump under her pillow. That's where she found the chocolate bar. An alarm went off in my head. Now I understood, that was the reason Rex snuck off and reappeared with a guilty look on his face. That Rex really is sneaky!

The last thing Brooke told me meant more than she'll ever know. She told me my "J" should stand for "Jumper". It seemed so simple but I finally had a response for that irritating question that came up so often. Now when people ask what my name stands for, I proudly tell them they can call me "Jumper". Sometimes, I even tell them how my cool big sister gave me the name.

That night was the last meeting of the Liberators held under the trampoline. The trampoline had been loyal but now had some missing springs and we had simply outgrown it.

We still have regular meetings only now they are held around the dining room table during dinner. Each meeting opens with a prayer and topics for discussion are never boring. We are currently seven members strong and holding. All seven members of our family. After all, like my parents always say, a family is a team, and no matter what, teams stick together.

ABOUT THE AUTHOR

  Sheila Rollins was born in Lexington, NE. She is the middle child with an older brother and younger sister. At the age of ten, her parents moved their family to Texas. She continues to live in Texas today where she is a teacher and has four sons and one daughter, who inspire her in everything she does. The family proudly stands by one another and Christ in everything they do.

www.ingramcontent.com/pod-product-compliance
Lightning Source LLC
Chambersburg PA
CBHW061314040426
42444CB00010B/2640